WHAT'S THE BIG IDEA, BEN FRANKLIN?

Ben Franklin was full of ideas about everything, from circulating libraries to electricity to wind-powered meat roasters. But he was much more than an inventor. He became the American ambassador to England, and when he couldn't talk sense to the English, he came home mad enough to fight them single-handedly! Instead, he helped write the Declaration of Independence. And then he went back to Europe (in a coonskin hat) to persuade France to be America's ally, and became a hero to the French.

What's the Big Idea, Ben Franklin?

by JEAN FRITZ

illustrated by Margot Tomes

Coward-McCann, Inc.

New York

Text copyright © 1976 by Jean Fritz
Illustrations copyright © 1976 by Margot Tomes
All rights reserved. This book, or parts thereof, may not
be reproduced in any form without permission in writing
from the publishers. Published simultaneously in Canada.
Printed in the United States of America

Library of Congress Cataloging in Publication Data
Fritz, Jean   What's the Big Idea, Ben Franklin?
Summary: A brief biography of the eighteenth-century
printer, inventor, and statesman who played an influential
role in the early history of the United States.
1. Franklin, Benjamin, 1706–1790—Juvenile literature
(1. Franklin, Benjamin, 1706–1790.   2. Statesmen)
I. Tomes, Margot   II. Title   E302.6.F8F88
1976   973.3.′092′4 (B)   75-25902
ISBN 0-698-20365-8   (hc.)
20   19   18   17   16
ISBN 0-698-20543-X (pbk.)
20   19   18   17   16

To Sue Sherwood

In 1706 Boston was so new that its streets were still being named. For 5 years the town officials had been thinking up names and they hadn't finished yet. So far they had Cow Lane, Flownder Lane, Turn Again Alley, Half-Square Court, Pond Street, Sliding Alley, Milk Street, and many others.

Luckily Milk Street had been named early, because that's where Benjamin Franklin was born. So right away he had an address. This was handy since he turned out to be famous and people like to know where and when famous men are born. (The day was January 17, 1706.) Of course no one knew then that Benjamin Franklin would be famous. No one dreamed that some day he'd have streets named after *him*. And towns, too. And counties, colleges, libraries, hotels, banks, ships, stoves, and stores. Even a football field would be named after him. And a flowering tree.

Certainly Benjamin's father never gave fame a thought. Mr. Franklin was a Leather Apron man; in other words, he worked with his hands and he had a trade. Carpenters, shoemakers, silversmiths, blacksmiths—all such men were called Leather Aprons because they wore leather aprons when they worked. Mr. Franklin was a soap- and candle-maker. His brothers were Leather Apron men and his sons would be Leather Apron men. That was generally the way it was in those days.

When Benjamin was born, his oldest brother, Samuel, was already a blacksmith. (The oldest son in the Franklin family was always a blacksmith.) Benjamin's brother James would be a printer. Three other brothers would be trained for the candle and soap business. The remaining four brothers died young. Two died as babies and Josiah and Ebenezer were drowned. Josiah ran away from home and was drowned at sea. Sixteen month-old Ebenezer ran away from his mother and was drowned in a tub of his father's soapsuds.

Benjamin was Mr. Franklin's 10th and last son. He was the youngest son of a youngest son of a youngest son of a youngest son of a youngest son—right back to his great-great grandfather. This made him special, Mr. Franklin thought. Besides, Benjamin was smart. Maybe he shouldn't be just another Leather Apron when he grew up.

No, Mr. Franklin decided, he shouldn't. Benjamin would be a preacher. He'd go to Latin School, then he'd go to college, then he'd climb up into a pulpit and make his father proud. So when he was 7 years old, off he went to Latin School. At the end of the year Benjamin was at the head of his class.

But he was only 8 years old. Mr. Franklin thought of all the years it would take to make Benjamin a preacher. And all the money! Besides, Mr. Franklin had been taking notice of preachers lately, especially young preachers in small churches. They had a hard time. Some went around with holes in their shoes. Now Mr. Franklin wasn't going to wait all those years and spend all that money just to have Benjamin climb up into a pulpit with holes in his shoes.

So he took Benjamin out of Latin School and put him

into an ordinary writing and arithmetic school for 2 years. When Benjamin was 10, Mr. Franklin took him out of school altogether. He was old enough now to run errands, to deliver soap, to dip candles. When he was 12 years old,

they'd decide what kind of a Leather Apron man he would be. Then he'd become an apprentice and learn the trade.

Benjamin didn't mind becoming a Leather Apron, but he did mind becoming an apprentice. And no wonder. An apprentice had to sign a paper saying he would obey his master until he was 21 years old; he would keep his master's secrets; he would be on duty as his master demanded both day and night. In other words, an apprentice lost 9 good years of freedom to learn a trade that Benjamin thought he could learn in far less time. And if there was one thing that Benjamin liked, it was his freedom.

So when he was 12 years old, Benjamin told his father that he might go to sea.

His father didn't care for that idea. Look what happened to his brother Josiah when he went to sea, Mr. Franklin said. If Benjamin didn't want to be an apprentice, he should stay home and go into the soap and candle business.

But Benjamin didn't care for soap and candles. Besides, look what happened to his brother Ebenezer in the soap-suds.

Of course Benjamin knew his father had a good business. His candles sold well. Even the night watchmen in Boston carried Mr. Franklin's candles on their rounds. And his soap sold well. Barbers said it made the best lather for shaving. Housewives said it was so mild that it could be used on scarlet cloth.

There was, however, one thing wrong with the business. It smelled. The hot stale grease that was used to make candles had a disgusting smell. The boiling lye that was used to make soap had a sharp, nasty smell and it stung a person's nose. Benjamin was determined he was not going to spend his life smelling those smells.

So Mr. Franklin took Benjamin to different shops to show him how hatters made hats, how cutlers made knives, how coopers made barrels. All these trades seemed interesting to Benjamin, but to learn any of them he'd have to become an apprentice. And Benjamin said no.

In the end, after much arguing, Mr. Franklin talked Benjamin into becoming an apprentice to his brother James, a printer. It worked out just as Benjamin thought it would. He learned the printing business quickly. And there he was. Stuck until he was 21. Being an apprentice to his brother was no easier than being an apprentice to anyone else. James thought Benjamin was vain (which was probably true) and argumentative (which was undoubtedly true), and he treated Benjamin as strictly, if not more strictly, than the other apprentices.

Benjamin could not bear to think of all those years going to waste. So he decided to use every spare moment to learn all he could about everything he could. He would read. He would write. He would observe. He would try out new ideas.

As a starter, he tried writing a poem. It was a long poem about the capture of Blackbeard the Pirate. He showed it to

THE CAPTURE OF BLACKBEARD   BY B. FRANKLIN A POEM

his father. Mr. Franklin thought it was a terrible poem. "Forget poetry," his father said. "Stick to prose."

To improve his prose style, Benjamin would read an essay, turn it into poetry, wait a few weeks, then turn the poetry back into his own prose. He found this increased his vocabulary. Later he would write letters to James' newspaper, signing them *Silence Dogood* so James wouldn't know he had written them.

Benjamin read a book on vegetarianism and decided to quit eating meat. He asked James to give him in cash half of what he had formerly paid for his meals. James agreed. Now Benjamin could not only eat by himself and read while he was eating, he could save some of his eating money and buy books. Many times a meal was only a biscuit, a handful of raisins, and a glass of water.

Once, Benjamin read a book about swimming that described unusual tricks and strokes. Benjamin was already an expert swimmer, but now he became even more expert.

17

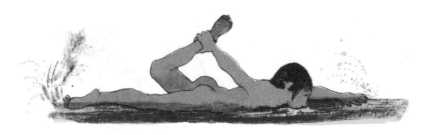

He learned to swim on his belly while holding both hands still, to carry his left leg in his right hand, to show both his

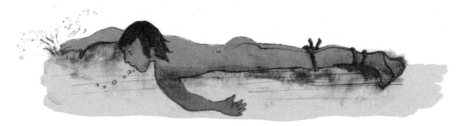

feet out of the water, to swim with his legs tied together, to sit in the water, to cut his toenails in the water, to show 4

parts of his body out of the water at the same time, to swim holding up one leg, to put on his boots in the water, and to leap like a goat.

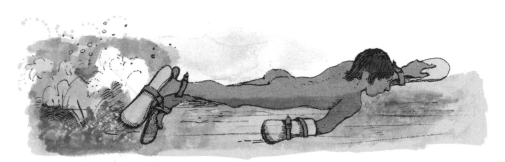

In order to swim faster he tried out an idea of his own. He made wooden paddles for his hands and feet. He went faster, but the paddles were so heavy that he didn't get far.

Then he tried lying on his back, holding a kite string, and letting the kite act as a sail and pull him across the pond. This was a great success. There was only one trouble. In those days boys went swimming naked. And if Benjamin didn't want to go home naked, he had to get a friend to carry his clothes to the other side of the pond. (It had to be a good friend because the pond was a mile wide.)

Benjamin studied arithmetic, which he had failed in his last year at school. He enjoyed it so much that in later years he made a hobby of constructing what he called magic squares. Here is one of his squares. Each row of 8 numbers when added up and down or across equals 260. Each of the 4 bent rows (as shown by the lines) also adds up to 260. The 4 corner numbers plus the 4 middle numbers add up to 260.

52	61	4	13	20	29	36	45
14	3	62	51	46	35	30	19
53	60	5	12	21	28	37	44
11	6	59	54	43	38	27	22
55	58	7	10	23	26	39	42
9	8	57	56	41	40	25	24
50	63	2	15	18	31	34	47
16	1	64	49	48	33	32	17

Benjamin also read a book on how to argue. The author said that a person should not flatly contradict another person. Instead he should be polite and ask questions until at last he had brought his opponent around to contradicting himself. Benjamin tried this and found that it worked.

He read a book by an Englishman with all kinds of advice. It told, among other things, how to catch eels, how to cure deafness, and how to keep horses from having nightmares.

Benjamin loved books that told you how to do things. He liked to figure out how a person could make work easier, life more comfortable, and at the same time get ahead in the world. He even read a book on how to be good and decided that being good was probably a practical idea.

Later he would make up a list of rules for good behavior: (1) Don't eat or drink too much, (2) Don't joke or talk too much, (3) Keep your things neat, (4) Do what you set out to do, (5) Don't spend too much money, (6) Don't waste time, (7) Be sincere, (8) Be fair, (9) Don't go to extremes, (10) Keep clean, (11) Keep calm, (12) Don't fool around with girls, (13) Don't show off. He kept a notebook in his pocket so he could mark down how he was doing. He didn't expect to be perfect. Each week he concentrated on one rule.

But Benjamin liked a good time and he seldom let his rules interfere. Once he spent 6 pennies to see the first lion ever brought to America. This was a lot of money, he said, but it was worth it.

Still, no matter what he was doing, Benjamin was always an apprentice. He couldn't forget it and he couldn't learn to like it. When he was 17, he could stand it no longer. He ran away. He boarded a boat and on one Sunday morning in October, 1723, he landed in Philadelphia, Pennsylvania.

He was free! He found a job with a printer and began earning his own money. When he had saved enough, he bought a new suit of clothes and a watch with a long gold watchchain. When he had saved some more, he went to Boston to visit his family. He dropped in at the printshop to see James. He didn't come to apologize for running away; he came, in spite of his rules, to show off. He swaggered into the shop, letting James and his apprentices see what a grand thing it was to be your own master in a new suit of clothes. He twirled his watchchain. He jingled the money in his pockets and offered to treat everyone to a drink. (James was so angry that it took years for the brothers to make up.)

Back in Philadelphia Benjamin was better behaved. He had a naturally happy disposition and made friends easily. Gradually he found other young men who liked to read and argue and try out new ideas. They formed themselves into a club they called the Leather Apron Club and met every Friday night. Each new member had to put his hand on his heart and swear that he loved mankind and the truth.

They talked about all sorts of subjects. Why, they asked, does dew form on the outside of a cold glass in hot weather? If the country has a bad law, should a man obey it? Can a poor man stay honest and still get ahead in the world?

Philadelphia suited young Benjamin perfectly. He lived on High Street, the busiest and noisiest street in town. On one end of the street was the Delaware River to jump into when he felt like a goat leap. On the other end of the street was Debbie Read, whom he courted and married.

Benjamin and Debbie were married in 1730. Benjamin was 24 years old now and getting ahead in the world. He had his own printshop, owned his own newspaper, and because he was such a good printer, he did the printing for the government of Pennsylvania. (He always used the blackest ink and the whitest paper he could find.) In addition, Debbie and Benjamin ran a store in the front of their house. They sold books, sealing wax, pencils, maps, pictures of birds and animals, fishnets, chocolate, compasses, codfish, and cloth. And they always had a good supply of Mr. Franklin's soap for sale.

Yet no matter how busy he was, Benjamin found time to try out new ideas. Sometimes he had ideas on why things happen the way they do. He wrote about comets. He formed a theory about hurricanes; they moved, he said, from the southwest to the northeast, contrary to the way winds usually move. Once he made an experiment with a pot of molasses and an ant. He hung the pot on a string and watched for the ant to crawl down. Soon there was a swarm of ants crawling up the string, so Benjamin concluded that ants have a way of telling each other news.

Sometimes Benjamin's ideas were for the improvement of Philadelphia. He formed the first circulating library in America. He helped organize Philadelphia's fire department. He suggested ways to light the streets, deepen the rivers, dispose of garbage, and keep people from slipping on ice in winter.

Sometimes his ideas turned into inventions. At the head of his bed he hung a cord which was connected to an iron bolt on his door. When he wanted to lock his door at night, he didn't have to get out of bed. He just pulled the cord, rolled over, and shut his eyes.

He invented a stepladder stool with a seat that turned up. And a rocking chair with a fan over it. When he rocked, the fan would turn and keep the flies off his head. He fixed up a pole with movable fingers to use when he wanted to take books down from high shelves. He cut a hole in his kitchen wall and put in a windmill to turn his meat roaster. And he invented an iron stove with a pipe leading outside. The stove produced more heat than an ordinary fireplace, cost less to operate, was less smoky, and became very popular.

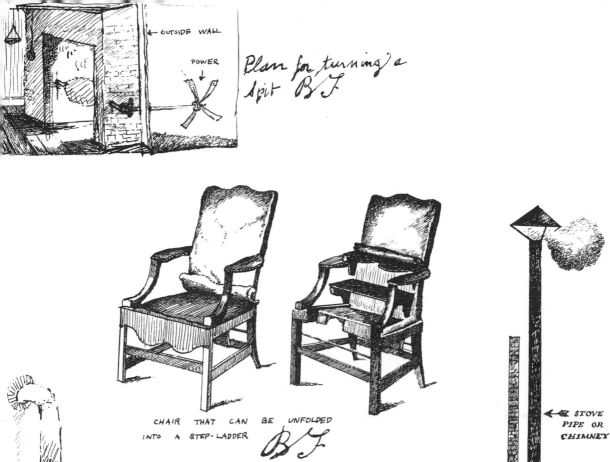

← OUTSIDE WALL

POWER ↓

Plan for turning a Spit B F

CHAIR THAT CAN BE UNFOLDED
INTO A STEP-LADDER
B F

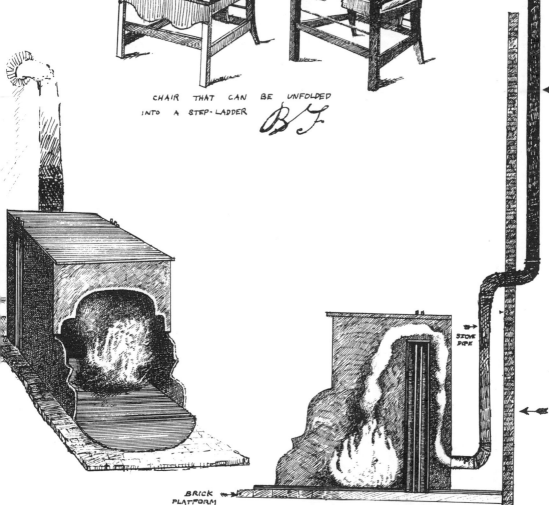

→ STOVE
PIPE OR
CHIMNEY

STOVE
PIPE

← HOUSE WALL

BRICK → PLATFORM
(CAN BE RAISED FROM FLOOR ON LEGS INSTEAD OF BRICKS)

In 1732, when he was 26 years old, Benjamin Franklin had one of his best ideas. He decided to publish an almanac. Every family bought an almanac each year. People read it to find out the holidays, the weather forecasts, the schedule of tides, the time the sun came up and went down, when the moon would be full, when to plant what. It was just the kind of book that Benjamin loved—full of odd pieces of information and bits of advice on this and that. It was, in addition to being a calendar, a grand how-to book and Benjamin figured he knew as many how-to's as anyone else. Besides, he knew a lot of jokes.

He put them all in his almanac, called it *Poor Richard's Almanack*, and published the first edition in 1733. His specialty was short one-line sayings.

Sometimes these one-liners were quick how-to hints for

everyday living: "Eat to live, not live to eat"; "A penny saved is a penny earned"; "Half Wits talk much but say little."

Sometimes his one-liners were humorous comments on life: "Men and melons are hard to know"; "There are more old drunkards than old doctors"; "Fish and visitors smell in 3 days."

In a few years Franklin was selling 10,000 copies of his almanac every year. (He kept it up for 25 years.)

This was certainly a good idea, but it was not Benjamin Franklin's Big Idea. He was 40 years old when he first became interested in the idea that would become the Big one. By this time he had 2 children—William Temple, who was 17, and Sarah, who was 2. (A third child, Francis, died in 1736 when he was 4 years old.)

The idea had to do with electricity, which had become a new fad. For some time it had been known that electricity could be generated by rubbing glass tubes with silk. Now a Dutch scientist had found that this electricity could be stored in specially equipped bottles, then drawn from them by applying wires (or conductors) to the 2 sides of the bottle. All over Europe people were meeting in darkened rooms to see these sparks and the tricks that could be performed. Wires twisted into the shape of giant spiders were electrified. Sparks were drawn from a cake of ice and

even from the head of a boy suspended from the ceiling by a silk rope. Electrical performers traveled from town to town selling shocks to curious people. Once, before a large audience in Spain, 180 grenadiers were linked together by wire, then given a shock to make them jump into the air at the same time.

Franklin bought electrical equipment and began writing to European scientists. He learned to perform the usual tricks and made up some of his own. Once he gave an electrical picnic. He planned to kill a turkey by an electrical shock, roast it in a container connected to electrical circuits, on a fire lit by an electrical bottle. He was, however, so carried away by his performance in front of his guests that he was careless. He took the whole shock through his own arms and body and was knocked unconscious. When he came to, he was embarrassed. "What I meant to kill was a turkey," he said. "Instead I almost killed a goose."

His Big Idea was that electricity and lightning were the same. Up to that time most people had thought lightning

was (and always would be) as mysterious as heaven itself. And here was Franklin saying it was the same stuff that you saw in parlor tricks—only on a grander scale. What was more, Franklin believed he could prove it. Let a sentry box be built on the top of a high tower, he wrote a scientist in Europe. Put a pointed rod in the tower and let a man stand in the box during a storm. Franklin knew that electricity was attracted to pointed iron rods; if the man in the sentry box could find that lightning was also attracted to a rod, that would prove they were the same. The only reason Franklin didn't make the experiment himself was that Philadelphia didn't have a high enough tower or even a high hill.

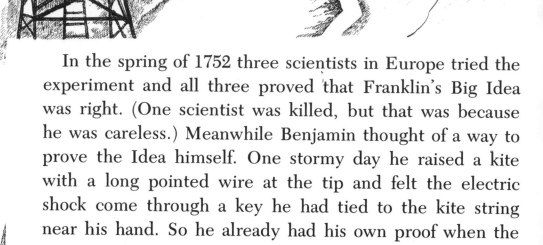

In the spring of 1752 three scientists in Europe tried the experiment and all three proved that Franklin's Big Idea was right. (One scientist was killed, but that was because he was careless.) Meanwhile Benjamin thought of a way to prove the Idea himself. One stormy day he raised a kite with a long pointed wire at the tip and felt the electric shock come through a key he had tied to the kite string near his hand. So he already had his own proof when the news reached him about the experiments in Europe. Still, he was surprised to hear how excited people were about his Idea. He was suddenly famous. Indeed, he was becoming the most celebrated man in America. The King of France sent him congratulations; the Royal Society of England presented him with a medal; universities gave him honors and called him Dr. Franklin; newspapers praised him. Benjamin was pleased. He felt secretly as proud, he said, as a girl wearing a new pair of garters.

A Big Idea, however, meant little to Benjamin Franklin unless he could put it to everyday use. So he invented the lightning rod, a pointed iron rod that could be raised from the roof of a house or barn to attract lightning and lead it harmlessly through a wire and into the ground. For his own lightning rod, he also fixed up a contraption that would ring a bell in the house whenever lightning hit. (Debbie hated that bell.)

Benjamin would have liked to do nothing but experiment with his ideas, but people had discovered that he was more than an inventor. Whatever needed doing, he seemed able and willing to do it. He was made Postmaster General and organized a new system so that it took only 3 weeks instead of 6 weeks for a letter to go from Boston to Philadelphia.

(Later he cut the time to 6 days.) He helped organize a fire insurance company, a hospital, and an expedition to seek

the Northwest Passage. And because he was so good at talking people into doing what he wanted them to do, in 1757 he was sent to London. He was to do what he could to further the interests of the people of Pennsylvania.

In London Benjamin began right away to live in style and comfort. He bought new shoes, new wigs, new shirts, a new watch, 2 pairs of silver shoe and knee buckles, new candlesticks, new chinaware, and a new carriage. He had his sword blade repaired and ordered new spectacles because he'd left his best pair at home. He rented 4 large rooms in a house owned by a Mrs. Stevenson, who treated him like a king. When his back itched, she gave him an

ivory backscratcher; she warmed his shirts before he put them on; she even trained her cat not to sit in his favorite chair. Of course she served only the foods he liked best (*never* beef, which upset him), and as if this were not enough, Benjamin received a regular supply of American cornmeal, venison, cranberries, and bacon from his wife, Debbie. (He sent Debbie presents in return, including a crimson satin coat and an apple corer.)

With the exception of 2 years back in America, Benjamin lived in London for 18 years, from the time he was 51 until he was 69. (Debbie, afraid to cross the ocean, died the year before he finally returned.) Benjamin was in London when George the Third was crowned King of England. He was there in 1765 when England began laying down taxes and making trouble for America. He did his best to keep the two countries friendly, but over the years England became more and more stubborn. First one tax. Then another. Sometimes England would repeal a tax, but it would never, never give up its *right* to tax America. Benjamin discovered that all his rules for arguing which had worked so well in the past were of no use against such stubbornness. He finally gave up arguing altogether one day in 1774 when he was called before the British government to explain his activities in behalf of America. For 2 hours he stood before the government's Privy Council. He was shouted at, laughed at, insulted, and condemned. Franklin, white with rage, said not one word. He was being treated like an apprentice. Indeed, England was treating America as if it were a country of apprentices instead of a country of free

men. And Franklin could stand it no longer. In the spring of 1775 he returned to America, only to find that America and England were already at war. The Battle of Lexington had been fought while he was at sea.

Franklin was so mad that he told Americans if there wasn't enough gunpowder to go around they should use bows and arrows against the English. He was so mad that he would have swum out into the ocean with electric bolts to shoot at the English, if he could have. But America had other uses for him. Right away he was put in the Continental Congress and placed on 10 different committees. When the time came to write the Declaration of Independence, he was one of those asked to do it. As it turned out, Thomas Jefferson did the writing, but Franklin made changes. The "truths" that Jefferson held to be "sacred and undeniable" became "self-evident" truths when Franklin had finished.

But these jobs were small compared to the big one Congress had for him. Benjamin Franklin was still America's best arguer and America's most famous citizen. So, in the fall of 1776, he was sent to France to try to talk the French into entering the war on America's side. George Washington would run the war in America, but Benjamin Franklin would run it in Europe, getting all the help and money from any country he could.

Benjamin was 70 years old now and found the ocean trip hard. The seas were rough; the weather was freezing. He had boils on his body, gout in his legs, and a skin disease on his head that bothered him so much that he wore a loose fur hat instead of his usual wig. When he arrived in France he was rumpled, crumpled, and weak—not the stylish, famous-looking figure the French had expected. Of course Benjamin planned to dress up as soon as he felt better, but

to his surprise he discovered the French liked him as he was, fur hat and all. Indeed, he was an immediate sensation. A plain man in the most fashionable country in the world! Within a month the French had made him their hero. French ladies found him charming. They fussed over him and called him Papa; they hung his picture over their mantels and wore his picture in their rings. Frenchmen cleared the way for him when he appeared in the streets. So Benjamin never did dress up. He never wore a wig or carried a sword the whole time he was in France, not even when he went to see the King. If being plain made him popular, Benjamin Franklin had the good sense to stay plain.

Paris suited old Benjamin perfectly. On one side he had the River Seine when he wanted a swim; on the other side he had friends when he wanted company. Altogether, Benjamin had such a good time in Paris that he couldn't always be bothered with his old rules for good behavior. Frequently he ate too much. But rather than worry, he carried a bottle of oil of wormwood for indigestion and he gained weight. (Sometimes he called himself Dr. Fatsides.) Occasionally he went to extremes. If he became interested in a game of chess, he'd stay up all night playing. And he wasn't neat. His desk was a mess. A Scottish visitor once pointed out the danger of leaving important state papers scattered so carelessly over his desk. There might be spies in the household, the Scotsman said. (And there really were spies.)

But the important thing was that Benjamin did what he'd set out to do. He talked France into joining America in the war and he took good care of America's business in Europe. And when peace came in 1783, he helped to write the peace treaty.

When Franklin (79 years old now) finally returned to Philadelphia, he was given a wildly enthusiastic welcome. Cannon were fired, bells rung, parades formed, speeches made. His daughter, Sarah, was so excited that she fell into

a wheelbarrow. But the people of Pennsylvania put Franklin right back to work. Three years in a row they elected him president of their government, and when Franklin was 82, they asked him to help write the Constitution of the United States. For 4 months he attended meetings of the Constitutional Convention. Sometimes he dozed off during a speech; often he disagreed with what was being done. But in the end he was satisfied with the Constitution. With so many different opinions, he said this was the best they could do.

Now at last Benjamin Franklin was finished with public life. He did not have long to live, but even when he couldn't get out of bed, he still read and he still wrote. And every afternoon his 9-year-old granddaughter, Deborah, would come to his bedside and he would hear her spelling lesson for the next day. If she did well, he would give her a spoonful of fruit jelly that he kept beside him.

At 11 o'clock on the night of April 17, 1790, Benjamin Franklin died. He was 84 years old—a man who had not only had a Big Idea of his own but had played a large part in one of the Biggest Ideas of his time—the idea of an independent United States.

7   Franklin Field belongs to the University of Pennsylvania and is in Philadelphia. Franklinia is a tree with a white flower. It is extinct now except for a few cultivated plants in Washington, D.C.

8   Franklin also had 6 sisters.

22   James Franklin could no longer legally claim Benjamin as an apprentice although he considered this only a technicality. Because of trouble with the government, James had been ordered to suspend his paper, but instead he made Benjamin the temporary editor. James had been forced to tear up the old apprenticeship papers but secretly had made a new contract just between the two brothers. Benjamin considered himself morally obligated to James but still when he escaped, there was no way for James legally to get him back.

24   Franklin gave up vegetarianism on the way to Philadelphia. One reason Benjamin visited Boston was that he wanted his father to set him up in his own printshop. Governor Keith of Pennsylvania had met Benjamin and had made this suggestion. When Mr. Franklin refused, the governor offered to raise the money and sent Franklin to London to buy the equipment. But the governor did not keep his promise. Benjamin stayed in London 2 years, working for a printer.

31   Later the Leather Apron Club was called the Junto.
     No one knows who William Temple's mother was. He was born before Benjamin married; Debbie became his stepmother.

34   The bottle was know as the Leyden jar.

36   Franklin was lucky that the bolt of lightning that hit the kite was not stronger. He could have been another dead scientist.

42   "We hold these truths to be self-evident," the Declaration says.
     William Temple went to London with Benjamin and later was appointed governor of New Jersey. When war came, he decided to support England instead of America. This was the biggest disappointment of Benjamin's life.
     Sick as he was on the trip to France, Benjamin Franklin kept busy with his scientific experiments. While the ship was crossing the Gulf Stream, he lowered a thermometer 2 to 4 times each day. Since it had already been found that ships which crossed the Stream directly made faster time than those which ran against it, Benjamin was helping to chart the Stream's exact location.

46   It is only fair to point out that Franklin had enemies in the American government as well as friends. John Adams, who worked with him in France, said Franklin was secretive and lazy.